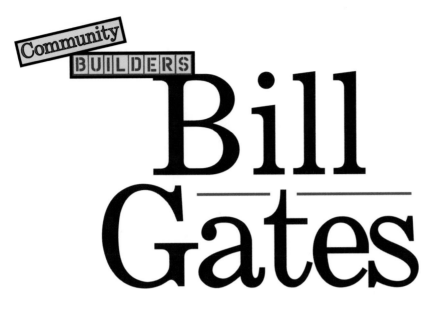

Community
BUILDERS
Bill
Gates

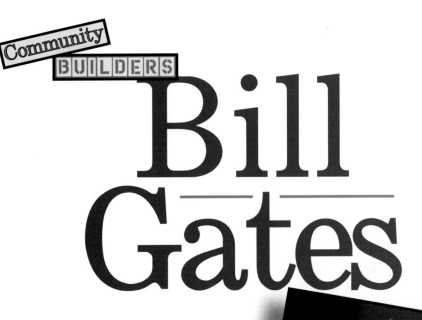

Community BUILDERS

Bill
Gates

Helping People Use Computers

by Charnan Simon

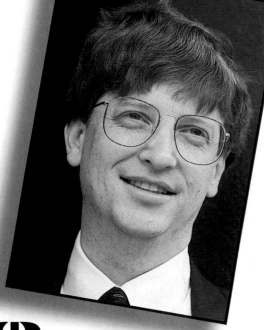

Children's Press®
A Division of Grolier Publishing
New York London Hong Kong Sydney
Danbury, Connecticut

Photo Credits

Photographs ©: AP/Wide World Photos: 8, 28, 35, 36, 40, 43; Corbis-Bettmann: 12, 22 top, 31, 44 bottom; Folio, Inc.: 2 (Matthew Borkoski), 24 (David R. Frazier), back cover, 3, 37 (Matthew McVay), 33 (Robert Rathe), 22 bottom (Dale Thompson); Lakeside School/Microsoft Archives: 13; Microsoft Archives: cover, 14, 19, 23, 25, 30; Monkmeyer Press: 26 (Paul Conklin), 44 top (Spencer Grant), 9 (Kagan), 15 (Rashid), 6 (Bernard Wolf); Seattle Post-Intelligencer: 17.

Author photograph ©: Tom Kazunas

Library of Congress Cataloging-in-Publication Data

Simon, Charnan.
    Bill Gates : helping people use computers / by Charnan Simon.
        p. cm. — (Community builders)
    Includes bibliographical references and index.
    Summary: A biography of Bill Gates, focusing on the Seattle business community and the global village that he has helped create through his work as a computer software entrepreneur.
    ISBN: 0-516-20290-1 (lib. bdg.)   0-516-26132-0 (pbk.)
    1. Gates, Bill, 1955—Juvenile literature. 2. Businesspeople—United States—Biography—Juvenile literature. 3. Microsoft Corporation—History—Juvenile literature. 4. Computer software industry—United States—History—Juvenile literature. [1. Gates, Bill, 1955-   . 2. Businessmen. 3. Microsoft Corporation. 4. Computer software industry.] I. Title. II. Series.
HD9696.C62G337 1997
338.7'610053'092
[B]—DC20   96-40964
                                                                                CIP
                                                                                 r97

Contents

Chapter One   *Computers and You*   7

Chapter Two   *"Anything I Put My Mind To"*   10

Chapter Three   *The Birth of Microsoft*   16

Chapter Four   *Computer Revolution*   20

Chapter Five   *Looking Toward the Future*   29

Chapter Six   *The Richest Person in the World*   34

In Your Community   44

Timeline   44

To Find Out More   46

Index   47

About the Author   48

Computers are a common sight in schools,
homes, and offices.

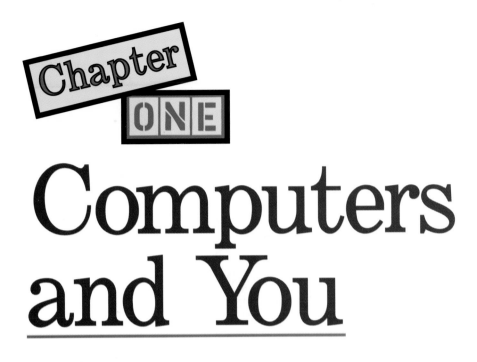

Chapter ONE

Computers and You

Do you use a personal computer (PC) at home or in school? What do you like best about computers? Playing games? Designing party invitations? Writing school assignments and sending e-mail messages?

You are not alone if you like personal computers, or PCs. Today, there are more than sixty million PCs being used in homes, schools, and offices around the world. Computers are everywhere!

A man named Bill Gates is glad so many people like PCs. Things were very different when he was growing up in Seattle, Washington. In those days, computers were too big and too expensive for ordinary people to own.

Bill Gates

Bill Gates thought everyone should have a computer. He knew that computers could help people in their homes, in their schools, and in their offices. With computers, people could work faster and communicate with each other more easily.

Computer Software

A computer cannot do anything by itself. It needs a program to work. A program is a list of instructions that tells a computer exactly how to do any given job. The general name for computer programs is software.

Stores carry different brands of software, but Microsoft is perhaps the most popular brand.

When Bill Gates grew up, he started a computer software company called Microsoft. He wanted to make it easier and more fun for people everywhere to use PCs. His dream for Microsoft was: "A computer on every desk and in every home, all running Microsoft software."

Today, Bill Gates's dream is coming true. Millions of people around the world use Microsoft products with their PCs. Microsoft has become one of the largest and fastest-growing companies in the world. And Bill Gates has become the richest man in the world. This is the story of how Bill Gates became the "Software King" and helped to bring personal computers to people around the globe.

Chapter TWO

"Anything I Put My Mind To"

Ever since he was a little boy, Bill Gates has liked to win. He was born in Seattle, Washington, on October 28, 1955. When Bill was growing up, he and his parents and two sisters used to play all kinds of games. Even then, Bill was serious about winning.

Besides being very competitive, Bill was very smart. He got straight A's in school—without ever taking home a book. "I can do anything I put my

Seattle, Washington

Seattle is the largest city in Washington State. It is nestled on the hills between Puget Sound and Lake Washington, in the northwest corner of the state. Seattle was founded in 1851. It was named after Chief Sealth, who was a leader of the Suquamish and Duwamish American Indian tribes. Today more than half a million people call Seattle home.

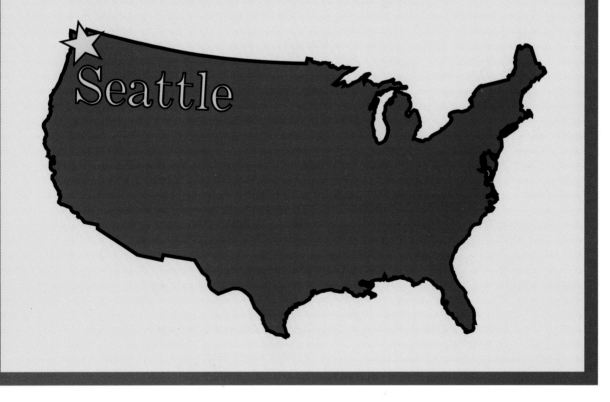

mind to," he explained simply. One thing Bill loved putting his mind to was computers. In the 1960s, computers were very different from the computers that exist today. They were so big that they filled a whole room. They were so expensive that only the government, large businesses, and some universities could afford them. There were no such things as personal computers for ordinary people to own.

Early computers were large, awkward machines that often required more than one person to operate.

Bill began writing his first programs while he attended Lakeside School in Seattle.

Still, Bill Gates managed to find businesses that would let him use their computers. After school and on weekends, he would work on the computers. Sometimes he got so wrapped up in what he was doing that he would work all night.

Bill learned so much about computers, he started writing programs telling them how to do complicated jobs. By the time Bill graduated from Lakeside high school, he knew more about computers than most grownups. He and his friend, Paul Allen, even started their own business using computers to earn money.

Bill knew that the future of PCs depended on the success of the Altair 8800.

After high school, Bill Gates went to Harvard University in Cambridge, Massachusetts. He didn't stay in college long, though. In 1974, he learned about a computer called the Altair 8800. The Altair 8800 could be built from a kit for only $399. It was small enough for ordinary people to use in their homes or offices.

Bill Gates thought this was the most exciting news he'd ever heard. This was the beginning of the computer revolution! Soon everyone could own a personal computer to help them do work and have fun.

But Bill knew that a computer all by itself wasn't very useful. A computer needs software programs to tell it what to do. Most people had no idea how much a computer was capable of doing. But Bill did. He knew that computers could be programmed to write reports and stories. They could be used to solve difficult math problems. They could design books, draw pictures, and play games. They could do thousands of jobs in homes, schools, and offices. But first, someone had to write the software programs that would tell computers how to do all these things. Bill Gates decided that he wanted to create new software.

This architect is using a PC to design a building, an impossible task for computers when they were first designed.

Chapter THREE

The Birth of Microsoft

Bill Gates didn't waste any time getting started. He knew that other people would also be trying to write programs for the new personal computers. Bill wanted to be the first person to succeed.

So, with Paul Allen, Bill worked around the clock for six weeks, writing a language program for the Altair 8800 called BASIC. When they were done, they flew to Albuquerque, New Mexico, where the company that made the Altair 8800 was located. It was time to sell their program.

Paul (left) and Bill (right) worked long hours to develop BASIC. Soon after, they established Microsoft.

Bill and Paul's hard work paid off. The Altair company bought their program, and the two teenagers were in business. Bill left Harvard University. He and Paul moved to Albuquerque to set up their own software company. Microsoft was born!

The BASIC language that Bill and Paul wrote for the Altair 8800 was just the beginning. Soon Microsoft was writing programs for new PC companies throughout the country.

It was an exciting time for Bill and Paul. They loved their work. Every new program was a challenge. Sometimes Bill worked sixteen or eighteen hours a day to meet these challenges.

Soon Microsoft had so much work, Bill had to hire people to help him. Many of these new programmers were friends that Bill had known in high school or college. Like Bill, they loved computers and were not afraid of challenges. Microsoft workers soon earned a reputation for working all day and all night if that was what it took to finish a job. Sometimes they even brought sleeping bags to the office!

18

By 1978, Microsoft had become so successful that Bill (front row, left) and Paul (front row, right) hired several talented programmers who worked as hard as they did.

Microsoft grew bigger and bigger. Finally Bill and Paul decided that the company was too big to stay in little Albuquerque. In 1978, Microsoft moved to the city of Redmond, Washington. Redmond is just 15 miles (24 kilometers) northeast of Bill's hometown of Seattle.

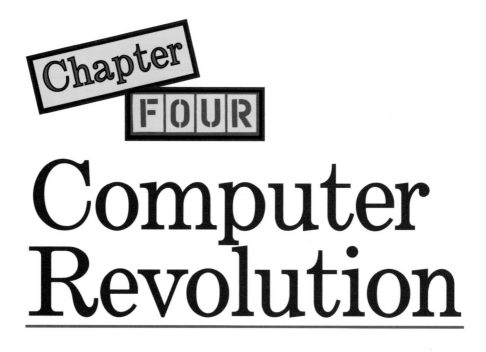

Computer Revolution

During the 1980s, the computer industry grew rapidly. More and more people in offices, schools, businesses, restaurants, and homes bought personal computers. There were more companies to make software and other products for these personal computers. Many of these software companies failed because the competition was so fierce. But Microsoft just kept growing bigger and more successful.

The year 1980 was especially sucessful for Bill Gates and Microsoft. A company called IBM (International

Business Machines) chose Microsoft to write an operating system for its new personal computer.

IBM was a leader in the business machine industry. It sold more different kinds of computers than any other company in the world. But IBM didn't sell personal computers. The company was being left behind in the PC revolution. So in 1980, IBM decided to catch up.

When IBM developed its new new personal computer, it needed an operating system. The company

Operating Systems

An operating system is a special kind of program. Without it, a computer can't run any other programs. An operating system is like a magic wand that wakes up a computer. It tells the computer: You are a computer! You have a keyboard, a monitor, and a printer! Use your power!

Top: IBM was a successful business machine company long before it began manufacturing PCs.

Right: A company called Wang made computers and software, but the tight competition resulted in the company's failure.

Introduced in 1980, MS-DOS quickly became the most popular operating system in the world.

turned to Bill Gates. Bill convinced IBM that Microsoft could give them just what they needed. But Microsoft didn't really have an operating system ready. Bill bought an operating system that another company had already produced. Then he put his Microsoft programmers to work. Soon they had fixed the system to suit IBM's specific needs. The operating system that Microsoft produced was a great success. MS-DOS (MicroSoft Disk Operating System) became the most widely used operating system in the world.

**Windows was the first operating system
to develop a mouse for use with PCs.**

Bill Gates had another big year in 1985. That year, Microsoft introduced the Windows operating system. Windows made personal computers even easier to use. Before Windows, people who used Microsoft systems had to type in commands for their computer. With Windows, they could use a device called a mouse to point to pictures to give commands.

24

Bill Gates had originally wanted Windows to be ready by 1983, but the program just didn't work right. He and his programmers kept working and trying to fix all the "bugs," or mistakes. Some people said Microsoft would never get Windows to work. But those people didn't know Bill Gates very well. After two years of hard work, Windows was finally ready. Just like MS-DOS before it, Windows quickly became a best-seller.

In recent years, Bill Gates has been devoting much of his time and attention to the Internet. He is

Microsoft Windows surpassed all expectations, and it eventually became more successful than MS-DOS.

The Internet

The Internet has useful sites for people of all ages.

When two or more computers are connected to each other, they create a network. If you work on a networked computer, you can take advantage of the power and programs of all of the computers in the network. The Internet (Interactive Network) is like a huge, global network. It connects more than sixty thousand smaller networks around the world!

For example, you can use the Internet to send electronic mail, or e-mail, to your pen pal in Australia in the blink of an eye. You can use the Internet to connect to NASA when you are writing a school report about the space shuttle.

excited by the many ways the Internet lets people all over the world share information and communicate with each other.

Bill Gates sees the Internet as being the next stage in the electronic Information Revolution. He believes that the Internet is a great way to encourage people throughout the world to live as a community. People can communicate with and educate each other over long distances. There's almost no limit to the ways that the Internet can be put to use. And Bill is making sure that Microsoft plays a major role in this revolution.

Paul Allen

Paul Allen helped to start Microsoft with Bill Gates in 1974. He left the company in 1983, when he became sick with cancer. Today, Paul is healthy again and serves on the Microsoft board of directors.

Bill Gates addresses Microsoft employees at the company's headquarters in Redmond, Washington.

Chapter FIVE

Looking Toward the Future

In 1974, Microsoft had just two employees—Bill Gates and Paul Allen. Today, Microsoft Corporation is the largest computer software company in the world. Almost eighteen thousand people work for Microsoft. In 1996, the company made more than $2 billion.

Microsoft is one of the Seattle area's largest employers. The Microsoft office buildings are

Microsoft's corporate campus is located just 15 miles (24 kilometers) northeast of downtown Seattle.

designed to look almost like a community of their own. There are thirty-five buildings spread out in a parklike setting, with a lake and many gardens. There are even baseball and soccer fields and volleyball and basketball courts for employees to use during their free time.

But Microsoft employees don't usually have much free time. Many of the people who work for Microsoft are a lot like Bill Gates. They're smart, they're hard-working, and they love computers.

Bill Gates encourages his employees to share their opinions. They can even argue with Bill if they think he is wrong. If someone disagrees with Bill, he will say, "Educate me on that." Because Microsoft is the most important thing in Bill Gates's life, he

Bill Gates prefers meetings to be friendly discussions where employees freely share their opinions.

wants it to be the most important thing in his employees' lives, too. He has not lost the competitive spirit he had as a child. He encourages his employees to come to work every day thinking, "I want to win!"

Not everyone likes Bill Gates. Some people think he is too competitive. They say he hasn't always been honest in his race to lead the computer revolution. Bill disagrees with people who say he is too competitive. All companies are competitive, he points out. Everyone wants their company to be the best.

"We win because we hire the smartest people," Bill told a *Time* magazine interviewer. "We improve our products based on feedback, until they're the best. We have retreats each year where we think about where the world is heading."

As a businessman and a computer whiz kid, Bill Gates has had an enormous impact on our world in the electronic age. Probably no one else has had a clearer picture of how computers would grow. It is impossible to think of personal computers without thinking of Bill Gates and Microsoft Corporation.

The influence of personal computers and Microsoft
Corporation has been felt throughout the world.

Chapter SIX

The Richest Person in the World

No matter how successful Microsoft becomes, Bill Gates shows no signs of slowing down. He still works between seventy and eighty hours a week (you go to school about thirty hours a week). He travels all over the world, talking about Microsoft and selling its products. He meets with other computer industry leaders to talk about new technology.

Bill (right) spends a lot of time traveling in the
United States and other countries, teaching people
about Microsoft and its products.

Melinda French Gates

Bill Gates has other interests these days, too. He and his wife Melinda have a daughter named Jennifer. They are building a new house on the shores of Lake Washington, in Seattle. This home will have an indoor swimming pool, a movie theater, a library, a boat dock—and computer technology everywhere. By the time the house is finished, Bill will have spent more than $40 million!

Bill Gates can afford such an expensive house. He is worth nearly $24 billion. But he knows that having so much money is a big responsibility. He would like to use his money in ways that will help the world. Right now he believes that he can help the world most by continuing to make Microsoft the best company it can be. Later, he will concentrate just as intensely on philanthropy.

36

**Bill Gates plans to devote as much attention
to contributing his fortune to worthy causes
as he has to the computer industry.**

Philanthropy

Philanthropy is caring for humanity by doing useful and helpful things. A philanthropist is someone who helps people, usually by giving large sums of money to worthy causes.

"Giving is a complex thing," Bill Gates has said. "You have to find things you really believe in and that are fun to give to. I take philanthropy very seriously and I am learning about it."

Bill Gates has already begun giving money away. In 1996, he was ranked third among the top philanthropists in the United States. He gave $135 million to worthy causes.

Bill especially likes giving money to schools and libraries. He has given $15 million to Harvard University for a new computer center. He has also given $34 million to the University of Washington in Seattle. And, he has given $6 million dollars to Stanford University in California. With his old friend Paul Allen, Bill Gates gave $1 million to build a new science center at the Lakeside School in Seattle that they both attended. When it came time to name the center, Bill and Paul couldn't decide whose name should come first. They flipped a coin, and Paul won. Today, the building is called the Allen/Gates Science Center.

Andrew Carnegie

A hundred years ago a businessman named Andrew Carnegie was the richest man in America. He was also a great philanthropist. One of Andrew Carnegie's favorite projects was building community libraries. Now Bill Gates is helping to bring these libraries into the global community of the Information Age.

When Microsoft's "Libraries Online!" program
debuted, Bill Gates hosted an online chat
with students throughout the country.

One of Bill Gates's favorite projects is Microsoft's program to give computers to inner-city and rural libraries. These libraries do not have a lot of money to spend on new books. But with computers, they can link up with the Internet. Through the Internet, they can use resources from libraries all around the world, just by clicking a button. Bill Gates is very excited by this idea. It's another way the electronic Information Age can make learning and communication easier than ever.

Whatever Bill Gates decides to do, either as a philanthropist or as the head of Microsoft, you can be sure he will do it with his usual drive and energy. "I choose every day to do exactly what I'm doing," he says simply. "There's nothing that's going to be as stimulating and have as much positive impact as this."

Bill Gates is sometimes called the "Software King." He has probably done as much as anyone in the world to shape the computer revolution of the last twenty years. He is now looking ahead to what might be called the "Internet Revolution."

For Bill Gates, the future is exciting. "I believe more than ever that this is a great time to be alive. The dawn of the Information Age offers the best chance the world has seen to make advances that improve the quality of life—or less grandly, merely to understand what is happening around us and stay in touch with families and friends, no matter where they are," he says.

**Bill Gates has been a leader
in the world's computer revolution.**

In Your Community

Bill Gates has seen his dream of bringing personal computers into homes, schools, and offices all over the world come true. He is dedicated to his company and has worked very hard to be sucessful.

What do you like best about using computers? Do you use any Microsoft programs at home or in

Timeline

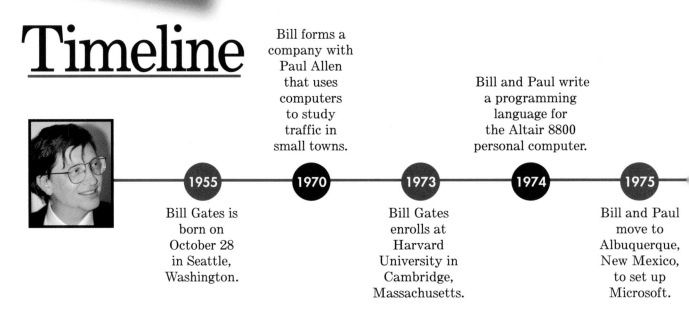

Bill forms a company with Paul Allen that uses computers to study traffic in small towns.

Bill and Paul write a programming language for the Altair 8800 personal computer.

1955
Bill Gates is born on October 28 in Seattle, Washington.

1970

1973
Bill Gates enrolls at Harvard University in Cambridge, Massachusetts.

1974

1975
Bill and Paul move to Albuquerque, New Mexico, to set up Microsoft.

school? Ask your parents, teachers, and librarians to help you find out just how many Microsoft products you use. Then send an e-mail message to Bill Gates. Tell him what you like—or dislike—about Microsoft products, or about computers in general. You can log on to *http://www.microsoft.com/corpinfo/bill-g.asp* to reach the site called the "Billboard."

Do you have any good ideas for new software programs that would make your PC more interesting or more fun to use? Tell Bill about your ideas!

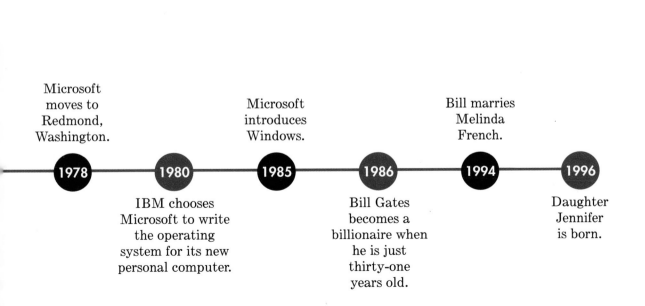

Microsoft moves to Redmond, Washington.

1978

1980
IBM chooses Microsoft to write the operating system for its new personal computer.

Microsoft introduces Windows.

1985

1986
Bill Gates becomes a billionaire when he is just thirty-one years old.

Bill marries Melinda French.

1994

1996
Daughter Jennifer is born.

To Find Out More

Here are some additional resources to help you learn more about Bill Gates, the Microsoft Corporation, and the Internet:

Books

Brimner, Larry. *The World Wide Web.* Children's Press, 1997.

Kazunas, Charnan and Tom. *Personal Computers.* Children's Press, 1997.

Simon, Charnan. *Andrew Carnegie.* Children's Press, 1997.

Zickgraf, Ralph. *William Gates.* Garrett Educational Corporation, 1992.

Organizations and Online Sites

American Institute of Philanthropy (AIP)
4579 Laclede Avenue, Suite 136
St. Louis, MO 63108

City of Redmond, Washington
http://www.pan.ci.seattle.wa.us/cities/redmond/redmond.html
Information about the city, its population, schools, businesses, and many other useful facts.

Microsoft Corporate Information
http://www.microsoft.com/mscorp/
The latest company news, online games, information about Microsoft's products and projects, and much more.

Philanthropy and Giving
http://www.zpub.com/aaa/phil.html
Links to different foundations and other philanthropic organizations, news, journals, and information about philanthropy in the United States.

Index

(**Boldface** page numbers indicate illustrations.)

Albuquerque, New Mexico, 16, 19
Allen, Paul, 13, 16, **17,** 18, **19,** 27, 29, 39
Allen/Gates Science Center, 39
Altair 8800, 14, **14,** 16, 18
American Indians, 11

BASIC, 16, 18

Cambridge, Massachusetts, 14
Carnegie, Andrew, 39
Chief Sealth, 11
computer revolution, 14, 21, 32, 41

e-mail, 7, 26

Gates, Jennifer, 36
Gates, Melinda French, 36, **36**

Harvard University, 14, 18, 38

International Business Machines (IBM), 20–21, 23
Information Age, 39, 41, 42
Information Revolution, 27
Internet (Interactive Network), 26, 27, 41
Internet Revolution, 41

Lakeside School, 13, 39
Lake Washington, 11, 36
libraries, 36, 38, 39, 41

Microsoft (Corporation), 9, 18, 19, 20, 21, 24, 25, 27, 29–31, **30,** 32, 34, 36, 41
mouse, 24, **24**
MS–DOS, 23, **23,** 25

network, 26

operating systems, 21, 23, 24

PC. *See* personal computer
personal computer, 7, 9, 12, 14, **15,** 16, 20, 21, 24, **24,** 32
philanthropy, 36, 38
programmers, 18, **19,** 23, 25
Puget Sound, 11

Redmond, Washington, 19

Seattle, Washington, 8, 10, 11, 19, 29, 36, 39
software, 8, **9,** 13, **15,** 16, 18, 20, 29
Software King, 9, 41
Stanford University, 39

University of Washington, 39

Windows (operating system), 24–25, **25**

About the Author

Charnan Simon lives in Madison, Wisconsin, with her husband and her two daughters. She is a former editor at *Cricket* magazine, and sometimes works at a children's bookstore called Pooh Corner. But mainly she likes reading and writing books and spending time with her family.

Charnan wrote this book on her eleven-year-old PC—a dinosaur in computer years. She uses one of the earliest versions of MS-DOS for her operating system and an ancient word-processing program called Multimate Advantage. Charnan has visited the Microsoft campus in Redmond and thinks it's beautiful.